STORYLINES

PARTICIPANT'S GUIDE
SMALL GROUP EDITION

STORYL|NES

PARTICIPANT'S GUIDE
SMALL GROUP EDITION

YOUR MAP TO
UNDERSTANDING
THE BIBLE

ANDY CROFT and MIKE PILAVACHI

DAVID C COOK™

transforming lives together

STORYLINES PARTICIPANT'S GUIDE
Published by David C Cook
4050 Lee Vance Drive
Colorado Springs, CO 80918 U.S.A.

Integrity Music Limited, a Division of David C Cook
Brighton, East Sussex BN1 2RE, England

The graphic circle C logo is a registered trademark of David C Cook.

The website addresses recommended throughout this book are offered as a
resource to you. These websites are not intended in any way to be or imply an
endorsement on the part of David C Cook, nor do we vouch for their content.

Unless otherwise noted, all Scripture quotations are taken from THE HOLY BIBLE,
NEW INTERNATIONAL VERSION®, NIV® Copyright © 1973, 1978, 1984,
2011 by Biblica, Inc.® Used by permission. All rights reserved worldwide. Scripture
quotations marked NLT are taken from the *Holy Bible*, New Living Translation,
copyright © 1996, 2007 by Tyndale House Foundation. Used by permission of
Tyndale House Publishers, Inc., Carol Stream, Illinois 60188. All rights reserved.

ISBN 978-0-8307-7873-7
eISBN 978-0-8307-7874-4

Adapted from *Storylines* by Liza Hoeksma
The Team: Ian Matthews, Jo Stockdale, Amy Konyndyk,
Nick Lee, Mark Prentice, Susan Murdock
Cover Design: Sarah Schultz
Cover Photo: Veer

Printed in the United Kingdom
First Edition 2019

1 2 3 4 5 6 7 8 9 10

051719

CONTENTS

WELCOME TO THE STORYLINES SMALL GROUP EDITION!

We love God's Word, but we know that it can feel intimidating and hard to understand at times. We wrote the book *Storylines* to try and help with that, to make reading the Bible more of an adventure than a chore, and to draw attention to the six overarching themes that run through it:

- Jesus
- Covenant
- Presence
- Kingdom
- Salvation
- Worship

Each of these storylines reveals a way of understanding Scripture and helps make it live and breathe, highlighting its relevance to our lives today. When we grasp these big ideas, and see how they develop and relate to the rest of the Bible, we start to view things in a whole new light.

Think of it like going on a fresh journey through the Bible with a new, clear, and well-lit path. The themes, or storylines, are our landmarks and together they give us the grand sweep of Scripture.

This resource is designed for your small group to take this journey together. It doesn't matter whether you are a brand-new Christian, engaging with God's Word for the first time, or have been following Jesus for ages and have read the Bible in its entirety many times; we believe this course will provide a fresh perspective for each and every one of us. It also doesn't matter if you haven't read *Storylines* itself; we've provided the key teaching on the DVDs and in this guide to help you get to the heart of the themes.

We hope you'll find this a helpful way to explore the overarching themes of the Bible as a group and that—more importantly—it will give you a clearer understanding of the God of the Bible, our amazing God who loves us in an incredible way.

Love from Mike and Andy

WHAT TO EXPECT

There will be six sessions that follow the six key themes of the Bible.

Your group leader will explain how the evenings will run, but it may look something like this:

- A time of prayer and/or worship.
- A short video with teaching from Mike or Andy.
- An opportunity to look at some of the key points of the teaching with your group, with time for discussion. As you will see from the material on the following pages we've split the teaching into small chunks with questions after each section and additional questions at the end. There are no right or wrong answers; this is a safe place to explore what you think and raise any questions you have.

After your group has met we would encourage you to continue exploring the themes that have been raised. To aid that we've included some pages in this booklet for you to journal and write down your thoughts and questions.

Though you may find it helpful, you don't need to read *Storylines* to be part of this group as we have summarised the key elements of teaching for you. If you would like to delve a bit deeper, the book (ISBN: 978-1-4347-6475-1) contains a great deal of additional teaching we hope you'll find helpful as well as lists of references to the relevant Scriptures each storyline is drawn from.

ABOUT MIKE AND ANDY

Mike Pilavachi is the co-pastor of Soul Survivor Watford in Hertfordshire, a church he planted in 1993, and the founder of Soul Survivor ministries, an international movement to equip young people to live every area of their lives for God. Mike is ordained in the Church of England and travels the world telling people about Jesus. He has a particular passion to see the whole church move in the gifts and power of the Holy Spirit.

Andy Croft is the co-pastor of Soul Survivor Watford alongside Mike, having first been one of his interns after he left school. They have led the church and Soul Survivor ministries together for many years. He is ordained in the Church of England, has a first-class degree in theology from Cambridge, is married to Beth, and they have three young boys.

Mike and Andy have written a number of books together: *Storylines*, *Everyday Supernatural,* and *Lifelines*.

THE JESUS STORYLINE

SUMMARY

From the very beginning God knew what a relationship with us would cost. He knew that God the Son would become one of us and give His life on the cross—this was no plan B. Astonishingly it's something God was willing to do! As if to make that clear, He hid clues and hints of this great salvation plan throughout the Old Testament.

Two thousand years ago Jesus said to the Pharisees, 'You study the Scriptures diligently because you think that in them you have eternal life. These are the very Scriptures that testify about me, yet you refuse to come to me to have life' (John 5:39–40). The Scripture Jesus was referring to was the Old Testament. At first glance it can seem the Old Testament is about Israel and Moses, David, Abraham,

Joshua, and others. Hidden in the background, however, like Wally in *Where's Wally?*, we find pictures of Jesus.

It's been said that Jesus is in the Old Testament concealed and in the New Testament revealed. We'd like to suggest that He isn't concealed very well! Not only are there 322 Messianic prophecies that point to Jesus, we also find hints of Him in the lives of many of the Old Testament heroes. In this session we will go on a journey of discovery, looking at how we see Jesus in the lives of Noah, Abraham, and Joseph. In the New Testament those hints, images, and prophecies are unveiled; the curtain is ripped apart, from top to bottom, to reveal the star of the whole show.

NOAH
GENESIS 6:5-8

The human race was messed up. They had turned from God and were doing terrible things to one another. God is holy and therefore could not have anything to do with them. But He had a problem: there was one righteous man, one who walked with God—Noah. A flood was coming, and God told Noah to build a very big boat and to make it out of wood. When the flood came, Noah's family got in the ark with him. Whilst everyone else died in the flood, Noah's family survived. This is a picture of Jesus.

God has found only one righteous human being—Jesus Christ. Jesus died on a wooden cross, our ark of salvation. Anyone who puts their trust in Him and becomes part of His family, even though they deserve to die, because of Him they will live. Even in the days of Noah, God was whispering Jesus.

QUESTIONS

What was it that meant Noah's relatives 'deserved' to be in the ark? Did they have to pass an exam to be his relatives? Did they have to be good?

What does this say about our relationship with Jesus?

ABRAHAM AND ISAAC
GENESIS 22

In Genesis 22 we find Abraham holding a knife over the chest of a young boy he's about to sacrifice. It was his son; a son whom he loved and who had been promised to him by God years earlier.

Now God was telling him to sacrifice Isaac. Why? The words He used in verse 2 are deliberately echoed in John 3:16, 'For God so loved the world that he gave his one and only Son.' God asked no more of Abraham than God Himself was willing to give. God gave up His only Son, whom He loved, completely out of choice and love for us.

There are other similarities in the two stories. For example, Abraham placed the wood needed for the sacrifice on his son's back (Gen. 22:6), and Isaac carried it up a hill in the region of Moriah. Centuries later, the Father placed the cross, the wood for the sacrifice, on the back of His Son. Jesus then carried the wood for His own sacrifice up a hill in the region of Moriah.

At the top of the hill, Isaac asked Abraham where the lamb for the burnt offering was (Gen. 22:7) and Abraham answered, 'God himself will provide the lamb for the burnt offering' (v. 8). Abraham then tied his son to the wood and was about to kill him when the Lord cried for him to stop. God told Abraham to sacrifice a ram he saw caught in a hedge. Rejoicing, Abraham took it and sacrificed it in the place of his son and 'called that place The LORD Will Provide' (v. 14). Two thousand years later on a mountain in the region of Moriah, the Lord provided a lamb for the offering ... the Lamb of God.

This provision of Jesus for us was something God had planned and intended from the beginning, before any of us were born. The storyline of Jesus running through the life of Abraham and Isaac shows us that God knew what was going to happen, and He knew what it was going to cost Him. He knew what you were going to cost—and then He went ahead anyway.

QUESTIONS

How does this knowledge that God was prepared to pay the ultimate price for you impact your life and your relationship with Him?

How might a greater knowledge of His sacrificial love change you?

JOSEPH
GENESIS 37-50

Jesus is everywhere in Joseph's story. Here are some of the similarities:

- Both men were born to rule. God revealed to Joseph in a dream (Gen. 37) he would rule over others. Jesus was born to be King, and because of His kingship many would find salvation.

- Joseph's jealous brothers sold him into slavery for twenty pieces of silver. Years later Jesus was sold to the Jewish leaders for thirty pieces of silver. Why is this so remarkable? The amount is exactly the same once you account for inflation!

- Joseph became the right-hand man to powerful Potiphar, and when Mrs. Potiphar tried to seduce him, he ran as fast as he could. Jesus was tempted in the desert by the Devil, who offered Him all the kingdoms of the world if only Jesus would bow down and worship him. In response to the Devil's seduction, Jesus said, 'Get lost!' (or words to that effect). Neither man would abuse the power entrusted to them.

- Joseph was unjustly thrown into prison, having been accused of a crime he hadn't committed. Years later Jesus was also accused of crimes He did not commit and was unjustly sentenced. While Joseph was serving his sentence, two criminals came to join him—the baker and the cupbearer. When Jesus was crucified, it was between two criminals.

- When Joseph was eventually released from prison, he became Pharaoh's prime minister, the highest position in Egypt. He said, 'God has

made me fruitful in the land of my suffering'
(Gen. 41:52). Egypt was an alien land that was
not his home. When God became man, He was
born into an alien land that was not His home,
and yet it was in this land of suffering that God
made Jesus fruitful. He was raised up from the
lowest point—death—and is now seated in the
highest, at the right hand of God.

- When Joseph's brothers came to Egypt to buy
food, instead of having them killed, Joseph
forgave them, assuring them that what they
intended for harm, God intended for good to
save many lives (Gen. 50:20). He saved the lives
of the brothers, who had sinned against him.
Jesus, as He was dying, cried out, 'Father, forgive
them' (Luke 23:34). We, the human race, meant
the death of Jesus for harm, but God meant it
for good. He intended it to accomplish what is
now being fulfilled, a passage from certain death
to abundant life, the saving of many lives.

This is more than just an amazing biblical parallel—it carries
with it a message for us today. God *planned* His death on the cross.
God always thought we were going to be worth it—His decision to
come to earth wasn't a last-minute afterthought. This picture is yet
another guarantee to our hearts of the love God has—and has always
had—for us.

QUESTIONS

Can you think of times you doubt God's love or feel unsure He'll do what He has promised?

How can you draw confidence from seeing Jesus' life foretold in Joseph's?

ADDITIONAL QUESTIONS

Are you surprised at the extent to which the Old Testament points to Jesus? If so, why? If not, then why aren't you?

....

....

....

....

....

What does this tell us about the way that the Old Testament links to the New Testament?

....

....

....

....

....

What practical relevance does this knowledge—that Jesus' life was foretold in so many miraculous ways—have?

> The *Storylines* book also covers how we can see Jesus in the lives of Moses and David, and takes a look at the many Messianic prophecies found in the Old Testament.

JOURNAL

Use the following pages to explore your thoughts around this topic and what stood out to you from your group discussions. Write down any further questions you'd like to explore and perhaps talk to someone about, and note anything you'd like to change in your life as a result of the things you've learned.

JOURNAL: SESSION 1

THE COVENANT STORYLINE

SUMMARY

The story of the Bible is the story of God pursuing the human race. Adam and Eve, as our representatives, turned their backs on God. Rather than walking away, God came even closer. God knows what every good counsellor knows: for a relationship to last, there has to be commitment.

'Covenant' is a type of commitment. The word might sound dry and technical, but at the heart of it is forming the kind of relationships that, deep down, we all need and want. The theme of covenant should not be of interest only to lawyers but to anyone who wants a relationship with God that is full of trust, security, vulnerability, and love.

The Bible gives us three key pictures of the covenant God makes with us. In the Old Testament (*testament* means 'covenant') the pictures are of the peace treaty and the marriage. Israel failed to keep their end of the covenant, and so God responded with an even more astonishing picture of His commitment to us. The New Testament shows us that the covenant God makes with us today is like a will. Because of what Jesus did, our name is written in God's will—there is an inheritance, and by God's grace it belongs to us!

THE PEACE TREATY

In ancient times peace treaties would often be made between a conquering king and the people he'd conquered. The king would lay down the terms for peace. The three parts of the peace-treaty covenant would be:

- The benefits to the conquered people (the protection and provision of the king).
- The obligations they would have (pay his taxes, obey his laws, and not swap him for another king).
- The penalty clause if they did not meet the obligations (he would withdraw his protection or punish them).

God made a similar covenant with Abram (Abraham, before God changed his name). God promised blessing or 'benefits' to Abram. He would make him into a great nation, and through his descendants the world would be blessed! Abram had obligations: he had to leave his country, his people—including his relatives—and go to a strange land that God would show him.

Years later, when Abraham's descendants became the people of Israel, this covenant was renewed with Moses at Mount Sinai. In this instance the benefits for Israel were that they became God's subjects. He would protect, nurture, and provide abundantly for them. The obligations Israel had were to obey God's law, worship Him alone, and not swap Him for another king. The penalty clause was that if Israel failed in their obligations God would withdraw His protection and allow them to be conquered by other kings.

Israel's story is one of repeatedly failing to fulfil their obligations. There were a few leaders who stuck close to God's laws, but most wandered away. They exchanged the God who'd made everything for little gods they'd made themselves. God sent prophet after prophet to call Israel back to Him, to remind them of the covenant, and to challenge them to repent and be faithful, but Israel refused. As a result God withdrew His protection, the people of Israel were conquered, they lost the land, they lost Jerusalem, and they lost the temple. The covenant was not to be taken lightly, and after hundreds of years of second chances, the penalty clause came into full effect. Israel went into exile.

QUESTION

In the picture of the peace treaty, we are to surrender to God's rule and not swap Him for another king. How might that look in our lives today?

....

....

....

....

....

THE MARRIAGE

The covenant theme captures the love affair that takes place between God and Israel. Nothing illustrates this better than the covenant picture of marriage.

When God brought His people out of Egypt and gave them His law, He in effect married them, declaring, 'I will take you as my own people, and I will be your God' (Ex. 6:7). The Bible uses the imagery of marriage to reveal and emphasise God's incredible passion for His 'bride'. Though Israel was unfaithful, God kept pursuing her, reaffirming His covenant—both with Moses and with David. In the years after David, when Israel went completely off the rails, God sent many prophets, not just to instruct her to obey the law, but to declare His love and beseech her to come back to Him. There's a reason the very first law is to love God!

One such prophet was Hosea. The book of Hosea is about a prophetic action: God told Hosea to marry and love an adulterous woman, probably a prostitute; someone he knew from the outset would break his heart. This was to illustrate the marriage of faithful God to unfaithful Israel, and how, even though it broke His heart, God could not bring Himself to give her up. God declared through Hosea His determination to bring Israel back to the heart of the covenant, to the place where they recognised Him alone as their God and themselves as His people.

Ezekiel is another of the prophets who paints this picture of marriage. Have a read of Ezekiel 16 to see how Israel's sin and rebellion broke God's heart, as well as His covenant. The unbelievable picture we have here is of a God who found Israel filthy, wretched, and abandoned, and rescued her, clothed her, and protected her. Then, when she was old enough for love, He covered her nakedness and in effect became her husband. He made her beautiful, giving her jewels and fine clothes. Then she used her beauty to prostitute herself in front of images she had made. She even killed the children He gave her in order to please these non-gods.

If we were God's marriage counsellor at this point, we would have said, 'You've given it your best shot. She'll never change and she's completely humiliated you. You've done everything you can to save this marriage. Now, for your sake, walk away.'

God didn't have us as His counsellor and He didn't walk away. When Israel failed to fulfil their obligations and the penalty clause came into effect, they were sent into exile. Exile was a hugely painful experience for the people of Israel, yet in the midst of this there came the powerful promises of God, giving fresh hope. In Jeremiah

31:31–34 He says He will make a new covenant. Rather than putting distance between us, God was going to come even closer. Significantly, He announced it would not be like the old covenant. What then was the new covenant going to look like?

QUESTION

What surprises you about what we learn about God through Hosea and Ezekiel?

THE WILL

The old covenant, based on a peace treaty and the picture of marriage, didn't work because the people could never meet the obligations. So what would be the basis of the new covenant? God couldn't water down the obligations, He didn't abolish the penalty clause—He would cease to be holy and just if He did. But He knew that whatever He did, we would never be able to meet the obligations and so, when it came to the new covenant, God didn't make it with us; He made it with Himself!

God the Son came to earth and became the only person who ever lived a perfectly faithful, loving, and righteous life. Where the old covenant had obligations, Jesus fulfilled them for us. Where the old covenant had a penalty clause, Jesus bore it for us on the cross. And where the old covenant promised the blessing of relationship with the Father, Jesus won this for us. In the new covenant, the Father and the Son shook hands. In Jesus, God had at last found His perfect covenant-keeping partner. The nature of this covenant is spelled out in Hebrews 9:15–17.

The picture that the New Testament gives of this covenant is the picture of the will. When a will is read, there are no obligations, there are no penalty clauses; it is simply about receiving an inheritance—who will get what. The basis of the new covenant is the last will and testament of Jesus Christ. A will is useless until the maker of the will dies. Jesus died on the cross, the scroll is opened, and we discover that the inheritance is ours! Everything that belongs to Jesus is ours (Eph. 1:3–8)!

What do we have to do? All we have to do is receive. We know what you're thinking: *It can't be this easy; there has to be a catch.* The amazing, spectacular, incredible, glorious good news of Christianity is that it is as simple as that. This is grace! Our salvation is a free gift, but one that cost Him everything.

So how does this affect the way we live our lives? It must change everything. This should bring an end to all our wonderings of whether we're in or out of God's kingdom by our own actions. We must put our faith in the facts and not our feelings. There is nothing we can do that will make God love us more, and nothing we can do to make Him love us less. To know this glorious truth is to be liberated from legalism and condemnation and to walk free as an heir of the King.

Can we ignore God's commands and do what we like then? No, we are to obey God, but our reason for obeying is not to earn anything (it's already all ours!)—it's as a response to His love and to express our love for Him.

This amazing truth is the foundation for everything else. The reason we can have such security is that God's love does not depend on us—it depends on Him. The glorious truth is He loves you, because He loves you, because He loves you. Never again doubt His love. Never again doubt your salvation. Your name is in His will.

QUESTIONS

Do you feel that the terms of the new covenant have sunk into your heart? If so, what are the effects of that? If not, what barriers in your life are keeping you from this understanding?

ADDITIONAL QUESTIONS

How might you live differently if you truly understood that God's love for you would never change?

....

....

....

....

....

What is the place of commitment in today's society, and what does it mean to you?

....

....

....

....

....

> If you'd like to read more, *Storylines* explores this theme of the covenant in greater detail.

JOURNAL

Use the following pages to explore your thoughts around this topic and what stood out to you from your group discussions. Write down any further questions you'd like to explore and perhaps talk to someone about, and note anything you'd like to change in your life as a result of the things you've learned.

JOURNAL: SESSION 2

THE PRESENCE STORYLINE

SUMMARY

This storyline is about understanding the astonishing truth that God wants to dwell inside of us! It's crucial for our understanding of both the holiness of God and His longing for intimacy with us.

Through this storyline we see the presence of God with humans from the creation of Adam and Eve, and how sin separated us, but God found a way to dwell amongst Israel. As the story unfolds, we see the tragic way Israel's sin left God with no choice but to remove His presence from the temple, but we follow the thread through to the incredible good news that God dwells in us through the Holy Spirit, and He promises that for eternity we will be with Him.

THE HOLY PRESENCE OF GOD

Adam and Eve were created to be in God's presence. In the garden of Eden they walked and chatted with Him in the cool of the day. After they had sinned, however, they hid from each other and God. The human race has been in hiding ever since.

Years later a fugitive called Moses came across a burning bush. God said to him, 'Take off your sandals, for the place where you are standing is holy ground' (Ex. 3:5). In Eden, Adam and Eve could spend time with God without worrying. After sin came into the world, God's holy presence now had to be approached with caution.

God is holy and so must set Himself apart from sin, but He also longs to dwell amongst His people. By giving Israel the law, God was saying the relationship is on His terms, not ours. The tabernacle is the place the presence of God Himself dwelt in the midst of His people. By placing strict regulations around the tabernacle, He sought to live among His people. He made a way to rebuild an intimate relationship with the people He loved.

QUESTION

How does the tension of God's holiness and His longing to be near us relate to what happened on the cross?

THE PRESENCE IS LOST

Since their time in Egypt, Israel had been repeatedly turning away from God. He had sent them warning after warning through prophets, trying to call His rebellious people back to Him. Ezekiel received visions of the temple in Jerusalem, with the people of Israel worshipping idols, sinning on the very doorstep of God's house.

In a spiritual sense, His home, the place on earth where He had chosen to dwell, had been violated. The holy God could no longer dwell in such a place, and Ezekiel had a vision about the glory of God—His presence—departing (chapter 10). It was as if God had been so scorned that He reluctantly packed His bags and left. It is because the holiness of God is offended that the glory of God leaves. God's address was no longer in Jerusalem, and the result was disastrous. The people of Israel thought their capital was indestructible, but in 586 BC, the king of Babylon crushed the city, destroying the temple. God no longer lived in Jerusalem; the presence of God had left.

QUESTION

In Scripture, when God's presence descends or leaves, people notice. What evidence is there in your life of the power and presence of God?

THE PRESENCE WILL RETURN … EVENTUALLY

Ezekiel went on to prophesy about the day Israel would return from exile. In Ezekiel 40–48, he has a vision of a new temple being built and the glory of the Lord returning to dwell among His people. This vision carries echoes of Eden; a river is seen flowing from the south side of the temple altar.

In the Bible, water is symbolic of life and particularly of the Holy Spirit. It's when the presence of the living God returns to the temple that life returns to Israel. As the river flows out from the temple in the vision, the dead land becomes rich and abundant, overflowing with goodness. Ezekiel tells us that 'where the river flows everything will live' (Ezek. 47:9) and prophesies that this sanctuary is to surpass the old one as it will be forever (Ezek. 37:26–28).

When we later read in Ezra about the temple being built, we hear that those who remembered the old temple wept when they saw the new one being built (Ezra 3:11–12). Why did they weep? Nobody knows for sure. It could have been that the older priests who remembered the first temple realised that something was missing, or rather Someone: this time there is no account of God manifesting His presence.

The glory fell at the dedication of the tabernacle in the wilderness, it fell at the dedication of the first temple under Solomon, yet it is notably absent in the dedication of the second temple (Ezra 6). But what of Ezekiel's visions? Didn't he predict that the glory would return? Didn't he tell us that a river of life would flow? Perhaps he had got it wrong … Enter Jesus.

QUESTION

What evidence do you see that where God's presence is there is an abundance of life?

EMMANUEL—THE PRESENCE IS WITH US

God the Son became a little baby. This is the astonishing truth of our faith! The eternal God who made the entire universe, the One who sustains everything—this God chose to no longer live behind a curtain in a building where only the chief priest could come once a year. Instead, He became one of us and walked among us. He was called Immanuel which means 'God with us' (Matt. 1:22–23; cf. Isa. 7:14).

The body of Jesus didn't carry God in the way a car carries a person. 'God with us' means God not just standing alongside us, but God becoming like us in every way—except that He was without sin. It wasn't that there was a 'God part' and a 'human part' to Jesus; He was totally God and totally human.

Even more amazing is that God didn't take on human flesh for thirty-three years and then dispose of it as soon as He had the chance. After the resurrection He invited Thomas to touch the wounds in His hands and the hole in His side. He ascended to heaven as a human, and when the dead are raised on the last day, heaven will be populated by human beings. At the moment there is just one man in heaven, and His name is Jesus.

QUESTIONS

What surprises you the most about Jesus being fully human? How does it impact how you relate to Him to think about the fact He experienced what it's like to live a human life?

THE PRESENCE LIVES IN US

Jesus, as He prepares to leave the world, tells His disciples, 'It is best for you that I go away, because if I don't, the Advocate won't come.

If I do go away, then I will send him to you' (John 16:7 NLT). When Jesus refers to the 'Advocate', a different translation is 'another like me' (see John 14:16). The unique, only-begotten, eternal Son of God talks about 'another like me'! This is because Jesus is speaking of the person of the Holy Spirit.

We believe in one God: Father, Son, and Holy Spirit. There is no simple way to understand the Trinity; here we must content ourselves with the understanding that each person of the Trinity is fully and equally God. Jesus is saying it is good news that He's leaving because whilst He (the presence of God) stood *next to* His disciples, the time is coming when the Holy Spirit (the presence of God) would *enter into* His disciples.

In the Old Testament the Holy Spirit comes upon prophets, priests, and kings. On the day of Pentecost the prophecy from Joel 2:28, 'I will pour out my Spirit on all people,' was fulfilled. The Holy Spirit is poured out on all of us!

What's more, the Holy Spirit changes us. From the day of Pentecost onwards, we see the disciples—a group of timid, fearful men who never quite seemed to get what Jesus was talking about—transformed into people who had boldness, power, authority, wisdom, and discernment. This was only because they were immersed in the Holy Spirit, because the presence of the living God came to live in them. It has always been the presence of God that makes the difference. *How utterly amazing: Almighty God lives in us*; we are His holy temple! If you are a follower of Jesus, then God lives in you too; you are a holy place.

QUESTIONS

Do you believe you have received the Holy Spirit? Why or why not?

Have you experienced or seen people being changed by the presence of the Holy Spirit like the disciples did?

THE KEY IS GOD'S PRESENCE

The key to Christian living is not how clever, good-looking, funny, well dressed, or connected we are. The key is God's presence. Moses discovered this when he protested that he wasn't eloquent enough to fulfil the task that God had given him. God's response was, 'I will go with you.'

After the death of Moses, when God commissioned Joshua to lead the people into the Promised Land, He knew Joshua was afraid. He didn't calm his fears by sending him a giant army; instead He said, 'I will be with you.' David, the most successful general and the greatest warrior in Israel's history, sings of the secret of his confidence: 'Even though I walk through the darkest valley, I will fear no evil.' Why? 'For you are with me' (Ps. 23:4).

A great theme in the story of the Bible is God longing and finding a way to be present among His people. Today the presence that used to walk around Eden, the presence that fell on Solomon's temple, the presence that every hero of the Old Testament sought, lives in us. The promise for the future is that one day His omnipresence, His manifest presence, and His indwelling presence will be one and the same, and in that presence all our sickness, our sorrow, and our tears will be wiped away (Rev. 21:3–4).

QUESTIONS

Can you describe a time you've experienced the presence of God most keenly? What impact did it have on you?

ADDITIONAL QUESTIONS

How could you make more space for God's presence in your life?

What has stood out to you the most as we've looked at the presence of God and why?

....

....

....

....

....

Storylines covers this thread in much more detail, including looking at the glory of the presence, how we're created to be in God's presence, the presence of love and holiness, and the power of the presence.

Everyday Supernatural by Mike and Andy also looks at the theme of living in God's presence and power.

JOURNAL

Use the following pages to explore your thoughts around this topic and what stood out to you from your group discussions. Write down any further questions you'd like to explore and perhaps talk to someone about, and note anything you'd like to change in your life as a result of the things you've learned.

JOURNAL: SESSION 3

THE KINGDOM STORYLINE

SUMMARY

The kingdom storyline is about understanding God's plan and our role in it. It begins in Genesis when we see God's intent for His relationship with His people. After Adam and Eve left Eden, we see God seeking to re-establish His kingdom by winning His people and giving them His laws, a land, and His presence. The Old Testament goes on to show the kingdom flourishing under the leadership of David and Solomon and then falling as subsequent kings disobeyed God.

Jesus burst on to the scene, announcing the kingdom of God. His life shows us many pictures of what God's kingdom looks like and who it is for. Today we live as agents of this kingdom, continuing to advance it even as we wait for Jesus' return and the final arrival of the kingdom in its fullness.

THE KINGDOM FORGED

The garden of Eden is always our picture of what God originally intended, and there man and woman had close fellowship with God. They had all that they needed in abundance, they lived under His rule and protection, and they were given authority over the whole earth. Yet they chose, by eating the fruit that gives knowledge of good and evil, to become independent. It was this choice that meant they were no longer able to stay in Eden; those who don't allow God to be their King can hardly expect to be part of His kingdom.

Because God loves us and His world, He set about re-establishing His kingdom. But for God to have relationship with us, He has to be our King; He is God, and He cannot be anything else.

To re-establish His kingdom, God first set out to win a people. In the book of Exodus we find the children of Israel ruled by Pharaoh and see how God had to fight two battles.

The first was the spiritual battle, taking on the gods of the Egyptians (Ex. 7–11). The Egyptians had some pretty strange gods, such as the frog, which represented the god of fertility. How does God deal with the god of fertility? He sends the frogs into over-drive. Suddenly there are millions of them—a plague all over Egypt. Another Egyptian 'god' was the river Nile. God kills the Nile. He turns it to blood, and it symbolically bleeds to death. The sun was the great god of Egypt, and that was blotted out by the darkness sent by the Lord. Pharaoh was regarded as a god in Egypt; the Lord killed his firstborn. Each plague was a victory in God's spiritual battle.

The physical battle followed. When Pharaoh sent his army after the Israelites and they came to the edge of the Red Sea, God parted the waters so the Israelites could cross safely. When the Egyptians tried to follow, the waters crashed down, killing them. Once the Israelites reached the other side, they joyfully sang a song of salvation that ends with the words, 'The LORD reigns for ever and ever' (Ex. 15:18). This was the first proclamation by Israel that the Lord was King. God had done it! He'd won a people!

Having won Israel for Himself and become their King, God gave them His Laws to obey (Ex. 19–20). The next thing He wanted to do was win a land for them.

The King led His people through the desert for forty years, and eventually they arrived at the edge of the Promised Land. The first city that stood in their way was Jericho. It was the Lord who won the victory; the walls of the city crumbled without the people firing a single shot (Josh. 6). This pattern was repeated again and again throughout the conquest of the land. Battles were won only when the King was with His people. He conquered a land for them.

QUESTION

The storyline of the kingdom is one of a battle between God and evil. In what way was the cross the ultimate battle, and what was it that Jesus defeated through the cross and resurrection?

THE KINGDOM FLOURISHING ... AND FALLING

The second great Old Testament picture of what the kingdom meant for Israel was the reign of David and his son Solomon (1 Sam. 16–1 Kings 11). The Lord chose to rule His people through an anointed son. David won lots of battles; while he and Solomon were kings, Israel did pretty well! They were the superpower of the region; their economy prospered and they lived in *shalom*, or 'wholeness'. The picture of the kingdom we see here is one of a kingdom battling and succeeding, a kingdom that hugely extends its boundaries and that has a wonderfully fruitful life under God's blessing.

Then ... disaster! Most of the kings after David and Solomon turned from the Lord. As a result God withdrew His protection and allowed the kings of Assyria and Babylon to invade and defeat His people (see 2 Kings 17 and 25). 'God's people' had lost their King. The Israelites now had nothing that marked them out as being subjects of King Yahweh. They were left to wonder if the King of heaven would ever return.

Then God sent prophets such as Isaiah and Ezekiel to say that He wouldn't only restore His kingdom; it was to be better than it had ever been before ...

QUESTION

What do you think a picture of God's kingdom flourishing today might look like?

THE KINGDOM FULFILLED

Jesus taught as much about the kingdom through His actions as He did through His words. Right at the start of His ministry, He read Isaiah 61 in the synagogue (Luke 4:18–21). He was announcing, firstly, that He was the anointed one—the Christ, the Messiah. Secondly, He was proclaiming what the kingdom would look like.

For the next three years the blind began to see, the oppressed were released, and good news was preached to the poor. What Jesus did showed what the kingdom of God would be like. For example, here are some of the things we see in Mark's gospel:

- In Mark 5 a woman who had been bleeding for years touched Jesus' coat and was instantly healed, then Jesus raised Jairus' dead daughter to life. He was the King who had authority over sickness and health, over life and death.

- In chapter 6 we see King Herod throwing a banquet and beheading John the Baptist. In contrast to the unjust king having an extravagant time with his elite guests, Jesus feeds five thousand in the wilderness. Jesus' kingdom is for everyone!

- The feeding of the five thousand also shows us a picture of the abundance of God's kingdom. Jesus miraculously multiplied a little boy's picnic, and after all had eaten, there were still twelve baskets of food left over.

- In Mark 8 Jesus feeds four thousand. It seems like a bit of an anticlimax after five thousand! But the feeding of the five thousand was in a Jewish area, the feeding of the four thousand in the region of the Decapolis (the Ten Cities), a predominantly Gentile area. This hints heavily that the kingdom was to spread beyond the Jewish nation.

- Jesus loses His temper when He walks into the outer court of the temple in Jerusalem and finds it has been turned into a market. The outer court was the place reserved for the Gentiles to pray, and market stalls would have made it difficult to focus on God. Jesus' kingdom was for everyone.

- After Jesus' resurrection He told the disciples, 'You will be my witnesses in Jerusalem, and in all Judea and Samaria, and to the ends of the earth' (Acts 1:8). The disciples were told to tell the whole earth that the King had arrived.

QUESTION

Which of these aspects of the kingdom would you most like to see more of in your life and for those around you?

....

....

....

....

....

THE NOW AND NOT-YET KINGDOM

If Jesus reigns, why are our own lives often a roller coaster? Some think that all the perfections of the kingdom are ours to receive now, if we have enough faith and obedience. Others think that though we have been 'saved', the kingdom of God on earth is wishful thinking; it won't be until we're in heaven that we receive any concrete sign of the King's reign. The teaching of Jesus and the whole New Testament is that we live in the kingdom now and not yet.

THE KINGDOM OF GOD IS NOW

Jesus said, 'The kingdom of God is in your midst' (Luke 17:21), a phrase better translated, 'The kingdom of God is among you.' He painted pictures of a dynamic kingdom emerging from a small beginning (seeds sown that yielded a harvest, of mustard seeds growing into huge trees, and a little yeast causing whole lumps of bread to rise). It was this small beginning, this carpenter from Galilee, that the Pharisees had missed.

Eating bread (Luke 14:15) and drinking wine (Mark 14:25) were signs of the kingdom of God. 'John the Baptist came neither eating bread nor drinking wine' (Luke 7:33), but Jesus arrived eating and drinking. Those who'd missed the fact that the kingdom of God was in their midst called Him 'a glutton and a drunkard, a friend of tax collectors and sinners' (Matt. 11:19; Luke 7:34).

Jesus clearly teaches through word and deed that the kingdom of God has arrived. The invitation He gives is that all who repent and accept God as their King will be welcomed into the kingdom with rejoicing. The words of Jesus echo through the Scriptures to us today—the kingdom of God is among us.

THE KINGDOM OF GOD IS NOT YET

In other illustrations Jesus told of a future feast, extravagant banquets and wedding feasts to which many are invited. This is a picture of the final judgement, the day when believers are separated from unbelievers (Matt. 22:1–14). We have received the invitation to the banquet now, but the actual banquet has yet to take place; Jesus has ascended into heaven, but He has yet to return as King.

The book of Revelation also contains a vision of the future kingdom of God. Then, 'God's dwelling place is now among the people, and he will dwell with them. They will be his people, and God himself will be with them and be their God' (Rev. 21:3). Furthermore, 'He will wipe every tear from their eyes. There will be no more death or mourning or crying or pain, for the old order of things has passed away' (v. 4).

Scripture tells us that the promised kingdom has arrived; it also tells us that the complete fulfilment of the promises of the kingdom is still in the future. If we say either that the kingdom has already arrived in all its fullness or that the kingdom isn't here at all, we miss the tension held in the Bible.

When Jesus died on the cross, the battle was won. We live in a time when, if we pray for healing, some people get healed; a time when some people become Christians; a time when God does bless us with His peace. On the other hand, some people don't get healed, many people are not remotely interested in Christianity, and we ourselves experience times of spiritual hardship. So why bother trying to live a life of the kingdom if the kingdom isn't yet fully here?

If Jesus is our King, we are to live to His standards. We are a people of the future kingdom of God, and if it's not good enough for the future kingdom of God, it's not good enough for the present. So when we see someone sick, we pray that God would heal them; when we see someone outside the kingdom, we invite them in; when we see someone in pain, we do all that we can to wipe the tears from their eyes.

The kingdom storyline began with the kingdom in Eden; it will end with the perfect kingdom in Revelation. We are called to live in the kingdom now and not yet.

QUESTION

Where do you see the tension of the kingdom now and not yet currently?

ADDITIONAL QUESTIONS

In light of this whole discussion, what do you now understand the phrase 'kingdom of God' to mean? Has your definition changed after reading this storyline?

Is God's kingdom around you? If so, where?

What does it mean for us today to be citizens of that kingdom? How does this citizenship change our relationship with Jesus and our relationship with the world?

> *Storylines* also covers the titles of Jesus and the ethics of His kingdom.

JOURNAL

Use the following pages to explore your thoughts around this topic and what stood out to you from your group discussions. Write down any further questions you'd like to explore and perhaps talk to someone about, and note anything you'd like to change in your life as a result of the things you've learned.

JOURNAL: SESSION 4

THE SALVATION STORYLINE

SUMMARY

The pattern is set in the book of Exodus and continues throughout Scripture; God is constantly intervening to save His people in all sorts of ways. God's plan of salvation, a plan that kicked in from the moment of creation, climaxed with a man dying on a cross.

On that cross God Himself displayed His justice and love through suffering on our behalf. He reconciled the world to Himself, restoring us to deep and intimate relationship with Him. He redeemed us to the point where we go from being slaves to sin to being children of God. And He won a victory that we could never win for ourselves. He defeated sin and He conquered death; He did it out of love for us and He longs for us to share in this victory. Without the cross and resurrection of Christ, there could be no salvation.

SALVATION IN THE OLD TESTAMENT

Though the storyline of salvation climaxes when a man is killed on a hill outside Jerusalem, the theme of God saving His people is present throughout the Old Testament. The story of the Exodus of the children of Israel from Egypt has been described as the 'controlling narrative' of the entire Bible—basically the story of the Exodus is echoed again and again through the Scriptures.

God saw the misery of His people, heard their suffering, and came to rescue them from slavery (Ex. 3:7–8). He disarmed Pharaoh and freed His people. On the night of their salvation from Egypt, the Israelites took part in a special meal: the Passover (Ex. 12). God told them to kill a lamb without any defect and smear its blood on their doorposts. Two thousand years later Jesus is described as 'our Passover lamb' (1 Cor. 5:7). When the people of Israel smeared the blood on their doorposts, God's judgement (in the form of the Angel of Death) passed over them.

When God sees the blood of Jesus on our lives, He passes over us, refusing to judge us as we deserve. So the salvation of the people of Israel from slavery in Egypt is itself a picture of the salvation brought about through Jesus.

God saved His people from Egypt and gave them laws to obey and instructions on what to do if they messed up. Israel often got it wrong, but whenever they turned back to God, He forgave them. When we read Judges, Kings, and Chronicles, we see Israel's history seems to go around in circles: Israel is in a good place with God; then they sin; then they are conquered by an enemy power; then they repent; then God saves them. The underlying theme of the Exodus is present here, in God's intervening to free His people from foreign powers. The same is true of the exile. When Jerusalem falls in 2 Kings 25 and the Jews are taken into exile by Babylon, God promises restoration. Just like the time He rescued them from Egypt, so too He will (and did) rescue them from Babylon.

QUESTION

Israel needed to be set free from slavery. If you had to express to someone why you need salvation and what difference it has made to your life (and you weren't allowed to use Christian jargon), what would you say?

THE CROSS

We can't get far as Christians without meeting the cross. Yet, for some of us, it raises questions. Was the cross necessary? If so, why? If God really is all-loving and all-powerful, why couldn't He just forgive us anyway? Where's the 'justice' in God punishing His innocent Son? What's it all got to do with the forgiveness of sins anyway?

On a purely human level, it's not difficult to pick out the reasons for Jesus' crucifixion. Jesus' popularity with the people, combined with His controversial teaching and actions, such as healing on the Sabbath, challenged the authority of the paranoid and power-hungry religious and political leaders.

Yet something much deeper was going on. The cross was planned by God, executed by God, and finished by God. It was as if God the Father said to God the Son, 'Your mission, should You choose to accept it, is to become one of them; to die on the cross; to take their sin, guilt, and shame on Yourself; and to bring them home.' Jesus—and this is important—chose the cross; it was not imposed on Him by humans or by His Father.

So why is the cross—an excruciatingly painful but also incredibly humiliating way to die—the only solution to sin? The Bible gives more than one answer to this question; it presents us with different 'windows' on the cross, and there are different ways of understanding this one event. If we don't look through the different windows, we'll miss the full picture.

QUESTION

What does the cross mean to you? Write it down, if possible.

WINDOW 1: THE CROSS AS PENAL SUBSTITUTION

This theological phrase is taken from the picture of the law courts. 'Penal' comes from 'penalty', so 'penal substitution' means a substitute paying the penalty, taking the punishment, in the place of the one who received the sentence.

Because of His holiness and requirement for justice, God cannot ignore sin, and Romans 6:23 tells us that 'the wages of sin is death.' The other half of the problem is that God cannot bear to look away from us because of His love. God can't ignore sin and He won't ignore us! The cross is the place where God's love and justice meet.

It was the human race who sinned, and so the human race had to pay the penalty. The entire human race, however, was sinful so God became a human being. And more than that, He became the only righteous human being. Jesus was the only one who could die on the cross because as both God and man He could display the love of God at the same time as paying the penalty for humanity.

WINDOW 2: THE CROSS AS RECONCILIATION

In any relationship, if there's a falling out, somebody has to make peace. You would usually expect the one at fault to be the one who has to make amends. Not so with God. He, the wronged party, came to draw us together with Him by making peace. Just as Jesus in His body, fully God and fully human, unites God and man, so Jesus in His actions on the cross brings together God and the human race.

When God looks at the cross, He sees our representative. Through His death on the cross, Jesus united God and humanity. The falling out in the relationship is dealt with and, wonderfully, we are reconciled to God. We get to share once again in intimacy with God (2 Cor. 5:18–19).

On the cross Jesus also made it possible for us to be reconciled to one another. We find the picture of this in John where Jesus looks down from the cross and says to His mother, 'Woman, here is your son,' and to John, 'Here is your mother' (John 19:26–27). Even on the cross Jesus was uniting people. The Bible tells us we are one in Christ; it's through Jesus' death on the cross that we are reconciled to one another.

It's because Jesus first loved us that we are able to love others as He does. This is a love that overcomes all barriers and heals all wounds. It is a love that focuses not just on our friends but on our enemies too. It is the love that Jesus displayed as He died for the people who were putting Him to death.

WINDOW 3: THE CROSS AS REDEMPTION

In biblical times the buying and selling of slaves was common practice. It was possible for someone to pay a 'ransom' in order to redeem a slave completely and set him free, which would have been an amazing gift. When the New Testament speaks of Jesus dying as a 'ransom for many' and bringing about our 'redemption', it is pointing to the cross as the answer to our slavery to sin. On the cross Jesus pays the price and sets us free.

It costs Him everything. He redeems us with His own blood. The result of this is not just that we are freed slaves—it's so much more amazing! God values us so much, so deeply, that He has redeemed us from slavery and adopted us as His very own children (1 John 3:1)!

WINDOW 4: THE CROSS AS VICTORY

When we think of victory, we think about strength, power, and domination. Jesus redefined victory. He won not by becoming stronger but by, on the cross, becoming weaker. He allowed Satan and us to do our worst to Him. While Satan thought that the cross was his greatest triumph, it turned out to be his ultimate defeat.

The victory of Satan lies in the fact that when he says 'you are not worthy' to sinful humanity, he's right. We are not worthy, we are guilty, we are sinful. The victory of Christ on the cross, however, is that we are made worthy. Jesus has taken all our sin, guilt, and shame on Himself. It has no hold over us. We are freed through His victory on the cross. So now when Satan accuses us, we don't plead our goodness but the righteousness of Jesus.

Jesus, referring to Satan, says, 'The thief comes only to steal and kill and destroy; I have come that they may have life, and have it to the full' (John 10:10). Satan's major aim was to separate us from God and to kill us by separating us from eternal life. Having suffered both sin and death, Jesus rose again to life! The resurrection of Jesus broke the power of death. Through His death and resurrection, Jesus won for us a relationship with God that will last for eternity. Jesus' final cry on the cross was, 'It is finished' (John 19:30). It is over; Satan has been disarmed and defeated (Col. 2:15).

QUESTIONS

Which window of the cross speaks to you the most? Why do you think that is?

ADDITIONAL QUESTIONS

Is salvation mainly something you understand in your head or your heart? Why?

Are you surprised the theme of salvation starts in the Old Testament? Why or why not?

Storylines also looks at why the cross was necessary, how our sin affected God, how our sin affects us, and how God's holiness and justice were satisfied through the cross.

JOURNAL

Use the following pages to explore your thoughts around this topic and what stood out to you from your group discussions. Write down any further questions you'd like to explore and perhaps talk to someone about, and note anything you'd like to change in your life as a result of the things you've learned.

JOURNAL: SESSION 5

THE WORSHIP STORYLINE

SUMMARY

God created the human race for a purpose: to live in relationship with Him. The relationship was intended to be defined by mutual love, and worship can be defined as the expression and outworking of our love for God. For our love to have depth, our worship must be more than just singing songs—specific acts of devotion are important but so too is a lifestyle of worship.

WHAT DO WE WORSHIP?

We can trace this storyline from Genesis. The heart of Adam and Eve's sin was choosing to turn from worship of God the Creator to worship of the creation. The biblical word for choosing to worship creation is *idolatry*, and this is the most common theme in the entire Old Testament. The greatest issue is not whether we worship; it's what we worship. When we stop worshipping God, we don't worship nothing; we worship anything.

We can read the pages of the Old Testament and feel smugly superior as we see the people worshipping things they've made—bits of wood instead of the Creator of the universe. The fact is, we haven't 'advanced' as far as we sometimes think.

Some of us have swapped the worship of gods called 'Baal' for the worship of gods called 'celebrities'. Instead of sacrificing to gain the favour of pieces of wood, we're now willing to pay the designer price that will earn us the approval of those around us. Given that worship can be defined as the expression and outworking of our love for God, it is fair to say that as the human race, we spend most of our time expressing and outworking our love for (worshipping) money, sex, fame, power, celebrity, one another, ourselves ... to name but a few.

QUESTION

Can you be honest about some idols that you struggle with?

ISRAEL'S WORSHIP

God's response to humanity's insistence on worshipping creation was given in Deuteronomy 6:5. He told the people of Israel, 'Love the LORD your God with all your heart and with all your soul and with all your strength.' The foundation of Israel's law was not a dry obedience to God but a life lived out of love for God. It's the difference between being a slave and being a lover: if you're a slave, you do it because you have to; if you're a lover, you do it because you want to. Both might get the job done, but they are worlds apart. Worship is the expression of Israel's love for God.

Worship was at the heart of Israel's life, and sacrifice was at the heart of Israel's worship. During every temple meeting, sacrifices were made. Sometimes it was an animal, sometimes it was grain, but every time it went up in smoke. They were offering tokens of creation, and by sacrificing them to God they were saying, 'You, the Creator, are more important than creation. You are more important than everything we have.'

One of the things Israel was doing when they made sacrifices was reversing the idolatry of humanity. But they messed it up. Even while Moses was having an amazing face-to-face encounter with God and receiving the Ten Commandments, Aaron and the people of Israel were busy making a golden calf to worship (Ex. 32).

The big issue about idolatry is not that it breaks God's laws but that it breaks relationship with Him. God is a jealous God, and idolatry is adultery. All the Old Testament prophets told Israel, again and again, 'You're messing it up; turn back to the God who loves you!' The problem was that even when they did sacrifice, they never managed to love God with their whole hearts. God wasn't looking for perfect sacrifices but perfect worshippers.

QUESTIONS

Does it surprise you to think of God as being jealous of your love and attention? Why or why not?

JESUS' WORSHIP

God looked all over the earth for one human being who would offer him perfect worship, but he couldn't find one ... until Jesus. Jesus lived a perfect life and then, on the cross, He died and offered an act of perfect worship to His Father.

Let's connect the dots. Hebrews 10:12 describes Jesus' work on the cross as offering 'for all time one sacrifice for sins.' For Israel, sacrifice was worship, so what our modern prayer books call the 'one perfect sacrifice' was the 'one perfect worship'. In Jesus, God found a perfect worshipper. He never sinned. In other words, He loved God perfectly, and this love was expressed through the whole of the way He lived his life.

Jesus' motivation for living was to please His Father (John 4:34; John 5:30). Jesus was the only human being in history who loved God with all His heart, all His soul, and all His strength. So when it came to the ultimate sacrifice, the cross, He was the 'one perfect sacrifice'. In His death Jesus didn't just choose the Creator over tokens of creation; He chose the Creator over life itself. Every second Jesus lived, and every moment of His death, was an act of perfect worship to God. Wow!

QUESTIONS

How does this help you understand what worship means? Is it broader or narrower than you previously thought?

OUR WORSHIP

So how do we worship? We don't need to sacrifice to make up for sin, as Jesus' sacrifice was 'once for all', but is there still a place for sacrifice in worship? Absolutely! We are told that, in response to the wonder and mercy of God, we are to give Him all that we are (Rom. 12:1). We are to worship with all that we do, not to earn love from God, but because of God's love for us.

Worship is so much more than singing songs; it is a way of life, it should involve all that we think and say and do. But it's also about specific acts of devotion. If it wasn't, the Bible would not repeatedly say of Israel that 'they worshipped.' When the magi came to the stable, 'they bowed down and worshipped him' (Matt. 2:11). After Jesus rose from the dead, the disciples worshipped Him (Matt. 28:17). In Revelation 4 and 5, we read that the four living creatures, the twenty-four elders, ten thousand times ten thousand angels, and the whole of creation will worship Him.

What does worship as specific acts of devotion look like? In the Bible it involves singing, clapping, dancing, lifting the eyes, lifting the head, lifting the hands, standing, kneeling, falling face down, and wearing sackcloth and ashes. Oddly enough it rarely involves just sitting!

Here are a few examples of this in the storyline of worship through Scripture:

- In Exodus 15, after Israel had been freed from slavery and escaped through the Red Sea, they praised. Salvation and singing go hand in hand! The first declaration by Israel that the Lord is King comes in this song (Ex. 15:1–2, 18, 20).
- The Psalms are full of commands and encouragements to sing and make music to the Lord.

From just Psalm 81:1–2 and Psalm 149:1–5, we see we're commanded to sing, shout, make music, dance, hit a tambourine, play the harp and lyre, and even to sing for joy on our beds!

- The New Testament doesn't give us a blueprint for how we're meant to worship, but it does say, speak to one another 'with psalms, hymns, and songs from the Spirit. Sing and make music from your heart to the Lord' (Eph. 5:19), echoing the principles we read in the Old Testament.

- Revelation 4 and 5 give us one of the greatest pictures of worship in the entire Bible and remind us of the object and reason for our worship: Jesus, the sacrificial Lamb (Rev. 5:6). If all our worship is not ultimately to Him, for Him, and about Him, then all the shouting, singing, banging, and playing is just a lot of noise.

QUESTION

What is a sacrifice of worship to you?

THE TWO-WAY LOVE SONG

Worship is a two-way love song. As we sing to Him, He rejoices over us 'with singing' (Zeph. 3:17). Throughout the Scriptures we see an inseparable link between worship and the presence of God. The link is this: worship is a response to God's manifest presence; it also ushers us into His manifest presence.

This link between the worship and the presence can be traced throughout Israel's history. When Israel lived in the wilderness, before the tabernacle was made and dedicated, Moses used to pitch a tent outside the camp, and when he entered, the presence of the Lord would descend in the form of a cloud (Ex. 33:10). Years later, when the temple was dedicated, worship and God's presence were again inseparably linked. We read in 2 Chronicles 5–7 that the people worship, God's presence falls, the people worship some more, God's presence falls again, the people worship again!

Worship is a response to the glory of God; there are few of us who would be able to stop ourselves from crying out praise should the weight of God's glory fall on us. These chapters in 2 Chronicles also show that worship has a place in ushering in the presence of God. We see this elsewhere, such as when the walls of Jericho fell after Joshua had the people worship (Josh. 6), and in Acts 16 when Paul and Silas were freed from prison after they prayed and sang hymns (vv. 25–26).

Worship is a response to the presence of God; it also ushers in the presence of God. And the power of God is in the presence of God.

QUESTIONS

Can you describe a time when you have known God's presence as you worshipped? How did it feel? Did it change you/your circumstances?

ADDITIONAL QUESTIONS

In the light of this storyline, what do you understand the word *worship* to mean? What evidence can we draw upon—both from Scripture and the world around us—to illustrate this?

Does worship change us? Why or why not?

If worship is for God alone, the audience of One, what practical difference could that make to our lives and church services?

Storylines covers this topic in much greater detail, looking at specific acts of worship throughout the Bible and exploring the link between worship and God's presence in more depth.

JOURNAL

Use the following pages to explore your thoughts around this topic and what stood out to you from your group discussions. Write down any further questions you'd like to explore and perhaps talk to someone about, and note anything you'd like to change in your life as a result of the things you've learned.

JOURNAL: SESSION 6